ALL
ABOUT
MYTHS

NORSE
MYTHS AND
LEGENDS

Anita Ganeri

Raintree

Chicago, Illinois

www.capstonepub.com
Visit our website to find out more information about Heinemann-Raintree books.

To order:
☎ Phone 800-747-4992
🖥 Visit www.capstonepub.com to browse our catalog and order online.

© 2013 Heinemann Raintree
an imprint of Capstone Global Library, LLC
Chicago, Illinois

To contact Capstone Global Library please phone 800-747-4992, or visit our website www.capstonepub.com

Edited by Nancy Dickmann, Adam Miller, and Claire Throp
Designed by Jo Hinton-Malivoire
Original illustrations © Capstone Global Library, Ltd., 2013
Illustrations by Xöul
Picture research by Hannah Taylor
Production by Victoria Fitzgerald
Originated by Capstone Global Library, Ltd.
Printed and bound in China.   042014   008200R

16 15 14
10 9 8 7 6 5 4 3

Library of Congress Cataloging-in-Publication Data
Ganeri, Anita, 1961-
Norse myths and legends / Anita Ganeri.
p. cm.—(All about myths)
Includes bibliographical references and index.
ISBN 978-1-4109-4973-8—ISBN 978-1-4109-4978-3 (pbk.)— ISBN 978-1-4109-6599-8 (ss)
1. Mythology, Norse—Juvenile literature. 2. Gods, Norse—Juvenile literature. I. Title.

BL860.G36 2013
398.209368—dc23   2012017719

Acknowledgments
We would like to thank the following for permission to reproduce photographs: Alamy Images pp. 7 (© Sindre Ellingsen), 21 (© Ivy Close Images), 23 (© imagebroker), 22 (© The Art Gallery Collection), 40 (© Mary Evans Picture Library), 41 (© Ivy Close Images); Corbis pp. 8 (Atli Mar Hafsteinsson/Nordicphotos), 15 (Felix Zaska), 17 (Werner Forman), 20 (Christophe Boisvieux), 37 (Werner Forman); Getty Images pp. 13, 14 (DEA/G. DAGLI ORTI/De Agostini), 36 (Jeffry Weymier); Shutterstock pp. 4 (©Arunas Gabalis), 6 (© Ozerov Alexander), 27 (© David Persson); SuperStock pp. 5 (David Lomax), 9 (Newberry Library), 12 (Clover), 28 (Douglas Houghton); The Art Archive pp. 29 (Richard Wagner Museum Bayreuth/ Alfredo Dagli Orti), 35 (Cavalry Museum Pinerolo/Dagli Orti); The Bridgeman Art Library pp. 16 (© Nationalmuseum, Stockholm, Sweden), 26 (Arni Magnusson Institute, Reykjavik, Iceland), 30 (Private Collection), 31 (Private Collection/ Photo © The Fine Art Society, London, UK), 34 (Private Collection).

Background images: Shutterstock (©3drenderings), (©Amy Johansson), (©StockCube), (©J. Helgason), (©Dm_Cherry), (©Dm_Cherry), (©Andreas Gradin), (©Algol), (©Triff).

Cover photograph of a stone Viking statue reproduced with permission of Getty Images (Duncan Walker). Cover graphic: Shutterstock (© Martin Capek).

The publisher would like to thank Roderick Dale of the Centre for the Study of the Viking Age at the University of Nottingham for his invaluable assistance in the production of this book.

Every effort has been made to contact copyright holders of any material reproduced in this book. Any omissions will be rectified in subsequent printings if notice is given to the publisher.

CONTENTS

Did you know?

Discover some interesting facts about Norse myths.

WHO'S WHO?

Find out more about some of the main characters in Norse myths.

MYTH LINKS

Learn about similar characters or stories from other cultures.

THE NORSE WORLD

The people who lived in Scandinavia from the 8th to 12th centuries were called the Norsemen, or sometimes Vikings or Danes. At first, the Norsemen mostly lived by farming, but they were also great raiders and explorers. From about 800 CE, they began to sail to other parts of Europe, raiding monasteries and towns for loot. Soon, they also began to settle in some of the lands they visited.

They were spurred on by a lack of good, fertile farmland at home. The Norsemen were brave and ruthless warriors, spreading terror wherever they went. However, they were also skilled craftsmen, and talented poets and storytellers.

MYTHS AND LEGENDS

Myths and legends are traditional stories. They are not based on historical fact but tell stories about gods and goddesses, supernatural beings, and events, such as the creation of the world and what happens after death. Since ancient times people have been telling these stories to help make sense of their lives and the world around them.

The Norsemen had a rich collection of myths, mostly describing the behavior and adventures of the gods. At first, the myths were passed on by word of mouth through storytellers, called skalds. They were often composed as poems, which may have helped the skalds to remember them. Later on, they were written down (see below).

Did you know?

The Norse myths were first written down in Iceland in the 13th century. The two main sources are called the Eddas, which retell the myths in poem and prose. The *Prose Edda* was written by the Icelandic scholar and politician, Snorri Sturluson, who lived from 1179 to 1241.

For how to pronounce Norse names, see pages 42–43.

The Norsemen sailed in ships like this one.

THE NINE WORLDS

In Norse mythology, the universe was made up of the Nine Worlds. These were arranged in three levels, one above the other. On the highest level were Asgard and Vanaheim, the worlds of the Norse gods and goddesses. Here, they lived in magnificent halls, roofed in gold and silver.

WHO'S WHO?

One god, Heimdall, had such good hearing that he could hear a sound as quiet as grass growing. He also had superb eyesight, was immensely strong, and needed very little sleep. Because of these special qualities, he was appointed guardian of Bifrost. He will blow his horn to warn the gods of the giants' approach at the start of Ragnarok (see page 41).

A rainbow bridge, called Bifrost, linked Asgard, the world of the gods, to Midgard, the world of humans.

MYTH LINKS

In Hindu mythology, the universe is arranged in circles around Mount Meru, the sacred mountain. The mountain is said to be made from gold and to be located in the Himalayas, the highest peaks on Earth. At the top are the cities of the gods. Further down are the continents and oceans. Below these are the underworlds and hells.

HUMAN WORLD

Below the worlds of the gods was Midgard, the world of humans. It was surrounded by an ocean so vast that no human could cross it. In it lurked the dreadful serpent, Jormungand, whose body circled around Earth. This middle level of the universe was also home to the giants and dwarves (see pages 30–31). Midgard was linked to Asgard by Bifrost, the rainbow bridge.

■ Midgard was the world of humans, where the Norsemen lived in settlements like this one.

LAND OF THE DEAD

At the lowest level of the universe was Niflheim, the land of ice, and Muspell, the land of fire. Muspell was the home of the fire giants. Niflheim was the Land of the Dead, a gloomy place of snow and cold that lay in permanent darkness. The Norsemen believed that those who did not die a brave or heroic death ended up in Niflheim. Niflheim was ruled over by the goddess Hel, a terrifying figure whose body and face were as black as a rotting corpse on one side but normal on the other. Niflheim's gates were guarded by Garm, a huge, ferocious dog with a blood-stained chest.

WORLD TREE

At the center of the Norse universe was a gigantic ash tree called Yggdrasill. It was so vast that all of the Nine Worlds were shaded by its branches or held in place by its three massive roots.

One root spread to Asgard, where it was tended by three women, called the Norns, who decided people's destinies. Another root reached into Jotunheim, realm of the frost giants. The third root stretched into Niflheim where a dragon, Nidhogg, gnawed at it constantly.

Did you know?

Icy Niflheim and fiery Muspell may have been inspired by the landscape of Iceland, where the Norse myths were written down (see page 4). Located far to the north, large parts of the country are covered in ice sheets and glaciers. There are also many active volcanoes, spurting out red-hot lava from cracks in the ground.

How the world began

Long ago, before the world existed, there was a place of ice and snow, called Niflheim, in the north. In the south was a place of fire and flames, called Muspell. Between the two lay a vast and gaping emptiness—this was Ginnungagap.

Eleven raging rivers flowed out of Niflheim and streamed into Ginnungagap, where they froze solid among the frost and wind. When the rivers of ice neared the glowing heat of Muspell, they began to melt and drip. From these icy drops, two creatures were formed. One was an evil frost giant, named Ymir. When he slept, he began to sweat, and from his sweat more frost giants were made. The other creature was a giant cow, named Audumla. Ymir lived by drinking Audumla's milk, while Audumla licked the ice for nourishment.

One day, as Audumla was licking the ice, the shape of a giant began to emerge. The giant was Buri, who in time had a son, named Bor. Bor married Bestla, a frost giantess, and they had three sons: the gods Odin, Vili, and Ve. Odin and his brothers hated Ymir and his cruel band of frost giants and, eventually, they killed him. Ymir's blood flowed out in torrents, drowning all the frost giants except two, who escaped in a hollowed-out tree trunk.

Odin, Vili, and Ve hoisted Ymir's body onto their shoulders, dragged it to the middle of Ginnungagap, and used it to create the world. They shaped Earth from Ymir's flesh and made the mountains from his bones. His teeth became the rocks and stones, and his blood filled the rivers and seas. His skull became the sky and his brains were tossed into the air as clouds. Finally, Odin, Vili, and Ve took some of the sparks and embers from Muspell and scattered them in the sky as the Sun, Moon, and stars.

GODS AND GODDESSES

The Norsemen worshiped many different gods and goddesses, who affected every aspect of their world and daily lives. In many ways, the gods were very like human beings. They fell in love, got married, fought each other, and had many extraordinary adventures. Unlike the gods in many other cultures, though, the Norse gods were not immortal. This meant that their lives were often in danger and they could be killed. Most of them were doomed to die at Ragnarok, the end of the world (see page 41).

This picture stone from Sweden shows Odin, the king of the gods, receiving warriors in his hall in Valhalla.

Did you know?

Very little is known about how the Norsemen worshiped. The only surviving accounts were written down about 200 years after their religion had died out and they had converted to Christianity. We do know that Norse chiefs may have acted as priests and that horses were sometimes sacrificed to the gods.

WAR BETWEEN THE GODS

The two main groups of Norse gods were the Aesir and the Vanir. They reflected two important sides of Viking society: war and farming. The Aesir were warrior gods and included Odin, king of the gods, and Thor, god of thunder. The Vanir were fertility gods who ruled over the sea and Earth. Norse myths tell of a long war between the two, during which the great wall surrounding Asgard (the home of the Aesir) was demolished. After the war, which ended in a truce, the wall was rebuilt by a giant and his magical horse.

■ Norse warriors and farmers worshiped the gods that were most important to them in their daily lives.

15

The theft of Thor's hammer

One morning, Thor woke up to find that Mjollnir was gone. Bursting with rage, he searched Asgard, but it was nowhere to be found. The other gods grew worried. Without Mjollnir, it would not be long before the giants stormed the walls of Asgard and brought the gods' world crashing down.

Loki offered to help find Thor's hammer. He borrowed the goddess Freyja's magic falcon skin that allowed the wearer to fly, and set off for Jotunheim, the land of the giants. There he found Thrym. Thrym admitted that he had stolen Mjollnir and hidden the hammer deep underground. "You can have it back," he chuckled. "If you give me Freyja as my bride."

Freyja refused. Luckily, Heimdall, the watchman, came up with a cunning plan. "Dress Thor up as a bride and send him to Thrym instead," he said, 'Loki can go as his bridesmaid! By the time Thrym realizes his mistake, Thor will have Mjollnir back."

The gods dressed up Thor in a long wedding gown with a thick veil to hide his face and beard. His goats were rounded up and harnessed to his chariot, then they raced off through a gap in the sky.

When Thor and Loki reached Thrym's hall, a great wedding feast had begun. Thrym showed Thor to a throne at the head of the table and sat beside him on another. "Help yourself to food and drink," he said.

As always, Thor was starving. In a flash, he devoured a whole ox, followed by eight whole salmon. Thrym had never seen anyone eat so much. Quickly, Loki explained that "Freyja" was so excited about her wedding that she had not eaten for a week.

Delighted, Thrym called for Mjollnir to be brought forward to bless the bride. But, as soon as Mjollnir was within Thor's grasp, he snatched it and ripped off his veil. Then he raised the hammer and killed Thrym with a crushing blow.

QUESTS AND ADVENTURES

Many characters in Norse myths went on great quests and adventures. One of them was Odin, king of the gods, who was also god of war and death. From his great throne in Asgard, Odin watched over the Nine Worlds. He was helped in this by two ravens that gathered news from around the Worlds, then perched on Odin's shoulders and whispered in his ears. Odin was married to Frigg, queen of the gods. Although he was stern and forbidding, he was also god of wisdom and poetry.

WHO'S WHO?

One of Odin's sons was Tyr, god of battle and law and order. The bravest god, he inspired warriors with courage in battle. Tyr is usually shown as a man with only one hand. The other hand was bitten off by a terrifying wolf, Fenrir (see page 34).

Sleipnir was the son of the god Loki. Loki gave the horse to Odin as a peace offering.

Odin's adventures took him to the other Worlds, often traveling in disguise and accompanied by two wolves. He rode on an eight-legged white horse called Sleipnir, which could gallop over land, sea, and air. Odin carried a magical spear, Gungnir, which never missed its target.

MYTH LINKS

In many of the world's myths, a hero or god undertakes a quest that tests his courage or strength to the limits. In Greek mythology, for example, the hero Hercules has to complete 12 seemingly impossible tasks, or labors, to make amends for the deaths of his wife and children.

Odin and the mead of poetry

When the war between them ended, the gods all spat into a huge jar to seal the peace. From this spit, they shaped a man called Kvasir. He became famous for his great wisdom.

Two evil dwarves invited Kvasir to a feast, where they killed him and mixed his blood with honey to make into mead. Whoever drank the mead would become a wise man or a poet. For years, the dwarves kept it a secret. Much later, they were forced to hand it over to a giant called Suttung. Suttung hid the mead deep in a cave under a mountain and set his beautiful daughter, Gunnlod, to guard it.

Before long, however, news of the magical mead reached the gods. "I will travel to the land of the giants to find it," vowed Odin.

Disguised as a giant, Odin made his way to a farm that was owned by Suttung's brother, Baugi. Odin tricked the farmworkers into killing each other. Then he went to see Baugi. "I can tend your farm," he offered. "A giant like me can easily do the work of nine men."

"How much would I have to pay you?" asked Baugi.

"Not much," said Odin slyly. "Just a tiny sip of Suttung's mead."

"Never!" Suttung roared, when Baugi asked him.

"Then," Odin told Baugi, "you can help me find the mead for myself."

Baugi led Odin to the mountain and bored a deep hole with his magic drill. Odin turned himself into a snake, slithered through the hole, and turned back into himself again. As soon as Gunnlod saw him, she fell madly in love with him. She agreed to let him have just one sip of the mead but before she could stop him, he picked up the cauldron and drained it. Then, keeping the mead safely in his mouth, Odin turned into an eagle and sped back to Asgard.

Sigurd slays the dragon

Long ago, a man named Fafnir killed his father and stole his huge hoard of gold. This gold had once belonged to the dwarf, Andvari, and it was cursed. The curse would cause the death of its owner, but Fafnir did not care. As his greed for gold grew, he turned himself into a dragon, so he would be better able to guard his trove.

Meanwhile, Fafnir's brother Regin brought up their nephew, Sigurd, as his own son. Regin forged a powerful sword for Sigurd, and the two set off to kill the dragon and bring back the gold.

Sigurd and Regin knew that they would need all of their cunning to defeat the dragon. First, Sigurd dug a trench across the path that Fafnir followed down to the stream where he went to drink.

"Wait in the trench, Sigurd," instructed Regin. "When Fafnir gets thirsty, he will crawl across, and you can kill him."

The ground soon began to shake as Fafnir came crawling down the path. In a flash, Sigurd drew out his sword and thrust it into Fafnir's body. The dragon was dead.

"Roast Fafnir's heart over the fire," Regin ordered. "I want to eat it."

Sigurd did as he was told, and to test if the heart was cooked, he poked it with his finger. The heart was hot and scalded him, so he sucked his finger to cool it down. As he did so, he swallowed some of the dragon's blood, and suddenly found that he could understand the speech of the birds twittering in the tree above him.

"There lies Regin," said one of the birds, "plotting to betray Sigurd and kill him so that he can have all of the gold for himself."

On hearing this, Sigurd drew his sword and cut off Regin's head. Then, taking a ring from the treasure trove, he set off on his travels and became the hero of many adventures.

The death of Balder

Wise and gentle Balder, the son of Odin and Frigg, had terrifying dreams about death. To make matters worse, there was a prophecy that he would be killed.

Frigg made everything in the Nine Worlds swear not to harm Balder. The gods turned this into a game. They hurled sticks, stones, and spears at Balder, but it was impossible to hurt him.

Only Loki was not happy. He was jealous of Balder, and hatched a plan to get rid of him. Disguised as an old woman, he visited Frigg.

"Is it true that nothing can harm Balder?" she wheezed.

"Nothing," confirmed Frigg, "except mistletoe."

At once, Loki went to find some mistletoe. He sharpened one end of a sprig to make a dart. Then he found Balder's blind brother, Hod, who wanted to join in the gods' game.

"I'll tell you where Balder's standing," Loki said. "Here's a nice, sharp dart."

Hod grasped the dart and fired it at Balder. It struck him in the heart and he fell down dead. A stunned silence fell over Asgard. Finally, Frigg spoke.

"Who will travel to Hel?" she asked. "To bring Balder back from the dead?"

"I will," said Hermod, Balder's brother, and galloped off.

The gods gave Balder a hero's burial. They carried his body to the sea and placed it on a great ship, piled high with treasure. They set the ship alight and pushed it out to sea.

In Niflheim, Hermod pleaded with Hel to bring Balder back to life.

"If every single thing in the Nine Worlds mourns for him, he can return," she said. "But if even one thing does not weep, he must stay here forever."

The gods sent messengers to every corner of the Nine Worlds, asking them to mourn for Balder. And everything began to weep… except one evil giantess.

So Balder remained in the Land of the Dead, and the giantess, who was actually Loki in disguise, was overjoyed.

CHARACTERS, CREATURES, AND PLACES

Look at the words in brackets to find out how to say these Norse names.

GODS AND GODDESSES

Aesir (A-seer) group of Norse warrior gods that lived in Asgard, including Odin, Thor, Balder, and Frigg

Balder (Bal-der) popular Aesir god and son of Odin and Frigg

Freyja (Fray-ah) Vanir goddess of love, beauty, and fertility; daughter of Njord and sister of Freyr; owned a magic falcon skin that allowed her to fly

Freyr (Fray-er) fertility god who protected warriors in battle; son of Njord and brother of Freyja; married to Gerd, a giantess

Frigg (Frig) queen of the gods; wife of Odin and mother of Balder and Bragi; visits Midgard in disguise to intervene in human lives

Heimdall (Hame-dall) Vanir god; guardian of Bifrost because of his super-sharp senses of sight and hearing

Hel (Hell) daughter of Loki; monstrous being, half alive, half dead, who rules over the Land of the Dead

Idunn (Id-doon) Aesir goddess; wife of Bragi

Loki (Lo-kee) mischief-making god; son of two giants and father of Jormungand, Fenrir, and Hel

Njord (Ny-ord) Vanir god and god of the sea; father of Freyja and Freyr; married to the giantess Skadi

Odin (Oh-din) king of the gods; god of war, battle, and poetry; married to Frigg; all-seeing and all-powerful

Sif (Siff) goddess of harvest and plenty; married to Thor

Sigyn (Sig-in) goddess and wife of Loki; faithful and loving, despite his wicked behavior

Thor (Thaw) Aesir god; great warrior, thunder god, and god of law and order; son of Odin and husband of Sif; defender of Asgard and archenemy of the giants

Tyr (Tewr) god of war; son of Odin

Vanir (Vah-neer) group of Norse gods; fertility gods including Njord, Freyja, Freyr, and Heimdall

GIANTS, DWARVES, AND OTHER CHARACTERS

Andvari (And-vari) dwarf who was forced to give his treasure to Loki but cursed it so that it brought death and misery to whoever owned it

Fafnir (Fahf-near) human who came into possession of Andvari's cursed gold; brother of Regin

Hrungnir (Hroong-near) giant who challenged Odin to a horse race and was killed in a duel by Thor

Regin (Ray-ghin) human and brother of Fafnir; brought up his nephew, Sigurd, to kill Fafnir and seize his gold; killed by Sigurd

Sigurd (Sig-urd) human and nephew of Fafnir and Regin; killed Fafnir and took his cursed gold; fell in love with the Valkyrie Brynhild

Skadi (Skah-dee) giantess; daughter of Thiazi and married to Njord

Thiazi (Thyah-zee) giant; father of Skadi

Thrym (Thrim) giant who stole Thor's hammer, Mjollnir, and paid for it with his life

Valkyries (Val-kye-reez) female warriors who served Odin and chose the bravest warriors killed in battle to go to Valhalla

Ymir (Im-meer) first frost giant who was killed by Odin; his body formed Earth

PLACES

Asgard (Ass-gard) home of the Aesir gods

Bifrost (Bee-frost) Rainbow bridge between Asgard and Midgard

Ginnungagap (Ghin-un-ga-gap) great expanse of emptiness that existed between Muspell and Niflheim before the world was created

Jotunheim (Yot-oon-hame) mountainous land that is home to the giants

Midgard (Mid-gard) home of humans

Muspell (Moo-spell) land of fire, guarded by the fire giant Surt

Niflheim (Niffle-hame) land of ice and darkness; location of Hel (Land of the Dead)

Valhalla (Val-hal-ah) Odin's hall in Asgard, where dead warriors feasted, fought, and prepared for Ragnarok

Vanaheim (Van-ah-hame) home of the Vanir gods

Yggdrasill (Igg-dra-sill) world tree; giant ash tree that held up the Nine Worlds

CREATURES

Fenrir (Fen-rear) monstrous wolf; son of Loki

Garm (Garm) huge dog that guards the entrance to Niflheim; ferocious, with a blood-stained chest

Jormungand (Yore-mun-gand) gigantic serpent; son of Loki

Sleipnir (Slape-neer) magical, eight-legged horse that belonged to Odin

GLOSSARY

chariot vehicle with two or four wheels that is pulled by a horse or other animal

compensation something given to make up for a loss, injury, or death

converted changed from one religion or set of beliefs to another

coyote animal similar to a dog or wolf that lives in the deserts and prairies of North America

dwarf in Norse myth, supernatural being created from maggots crawling on the body of the giant, Ymir. Dwarves are skilled craftsmen who live under the ground.

fertile able to produce new life, new plants, or animals

fertility ability to produce new life, new plants, or animals

forged when metal is heated and hammered to make weapons and tools

giant in Norse myth, supernatural being who is the enemy of the gods. Giants are enormously strong and able to change shape.

glacier huge river of ice that flows down mountains into the sea

guardian someone who looks after, protects, or defends a place

Hindu relating to the Hindu religion, which began in India more than 4,000 years ago

hostage person held as security to make sure that a promise is kept

immortal living forever; describes a being who cannot be killed

lava red-hot, liquid rock that bursts from the ground when a volcano erupts

maize plant that is also known as sweet corn

mead strong drink made using honey

mistletoe plant with waxy white berries that often grows on oak trees

Mjollnir (Myoll-neer) Thor's hammer, which was made by the dwarves

prophecy prediction of what will happen in the future

prophetess woman who makes a prophecy

prose spoken or written language that is not poetical

quest long, difficult search for something

Ragnarok (Rag-na-rock) great battle between the gods and giants at the end of the world

rune character in the Norse alphabet

sacrificed killed and offered to the gods to earn their favor or goodwill

skald professional poet in Norse society

source place where information comes from. This may be a person, an object, or a book.

supernatural describes beings or events that cannot be explained by natural or scientific laws

trickster character in myths who plays tricks and makes mischief

truce agreement to stop fighting during a war

whetstone stone used for sharpening knives and other tools

FIND OUT MORE

BOOKS

Lunge-Larsen, Lise. *The Adventures of Thor the Thunder God*. New York: Houghton Mifflin, 2007.

Margeson, Susan. *Viking* (DK Eyewitness Books). New York: DK Children, 2009.

MacDonald, Fiona. *100 Things You Should Know About Vikings*. Broomall, Pa.: Mason Crest, 2010.

Ollhof, Jim. *Norse Mythology* (The World of Mythology). Minneapolis: ABDO and Daughters, 2011.

Schomp, Virginia. *The Norsemen* (Myths of the World). New York: Benchmark Books, 2007.

WEB SITES

www.bbc.co.uk/history/ancient/vikings
This BBC web site investigates the lives of the Vikings (Norsemen) and the evidence for what we know about their culture.

www.bbc.co.uk/history/handsonhistory/vikings.shtml
This humorous, animated BBC web site about the Vikings allows you to step back in time and make your own Viking longship.

www.mnh.si.edu/vikings/start.html
Take a guided tour of the Smithsonian National Museum of Natural History exhibit called "Vikings: The North Atlantic Saga."

www.pbs.org/wgbh/nova/vikings/
This web site is a companion to a PBS NOVA special on the Vikings. Explore a Viking village and learn more about Viking culture.

PLACES TO VISIT

Jorvik Viking Centre
York, England
www.jorvik-viking-centre.co.uk
The Jorvik Viking Centre stands on the site of a 1,000-year-old Viking settlement excavated in the city of York, England. You can experience what it was like to live in a Viking town.

The Viking Ship Museum
Oslo, Norway
www.khm.uio.no/vikingskipshuset/index_eng.html
This amazing museum houses several complete or nearly complete Viking longships and many other artifacts.

The Viking Ship Museum
Roskilde, Denmark
www.vikingeskibsmuseet.dk/en
Visit the museum to see five reconstructed Viking ships, get the chance to go sailing in a longship, and find out how the ships were built.

FURTHER RESEARCH

Which Norse myth did you like reading most in this book? Which characters did you find most interesting? Can you find out about any more myths in which these characters appear? You could look in the books or on the web sites given on page 46, or even visit some of the places mentioned above. You could also try retelling your favorite myth in new way, such as in a diary, a cartoon strip, or a newspaper report.

INDEX